Rising from the Ashes

RISING
FROM THE ASHES

The Chimney Tops 2 Wildfires in Memory and Art

ILLUSTRATIONS BY

Paige Braddock, Charlie Daniel, Marshall Ramsey, and Danny Wilson

TEXT BY

Stephen Lyn Bales

Contents

Illustrations

Foreword

THE ILLUSTRATIONS FEATURED IN THIS CATALOG SPRING FROM
a larger project to document through oral-history interviews the experiences
of individuals involved in or impacted by the terrible wildfires that ravaged the
Great Smoky Mountains near Gatlinburg, Tennessee, in November of 2016.
Considered one of the worst natural disasters in Tennessee's history and the
largest wildfire on the East Coast in more than fifty years, the fires caused
injuries and fatalities, destroyed and damaged homes and businesses,
impacted wildlife, and left thousands of acres burned and charred.

Rising from the Ashes: The Chimney Tops 2 Wildfires Oral History Project
began as a three-year initiative in 2019 by the University of Tennessee
Libraries in partnership with the City of Gatlinburg and the Anna Porter Public
Library. At the outset of the project, the Anna Porter Public Library generously
donated forty-six audio interviews its staff and volunteers had collected
immediately after the fires. Over the last three years, members of the Rising
from the Ashes (RFTA) team conducted around one hundred more interviews,
most of them in audiovisual format. The oral histories include interviews with
those who lost homes and businesses, first responders, recovery specialists

and representatives from charitable and volunteer organizations, government officials, fire and forestry experts, scientists, environmentalists, artists, lawyers, journalists, clergy, mental health professionals, educators, and many others. The interviews are preserved for posterity in the UT Libraries' Betsey B. Creekmore Special Collections and University Archives and have been made available online with descriptive metadata and transcripts at https://rfta.lib.utk.edu/. Interviews conducted in Spanish include English translations.

Early in the project the RFTA team applied for a National Endowment for the Arts (NEA) grant through its creative placemaking Our Town program, which seeks to strengthen communities through projects involving arts, culture, and design to advance "economic, physical, and/or social outcomes." In conducting the interviews, many of the narrators shared with the team the therapeutic and even cathartic effect of documenting their experiences as part of the oral history archive. The team felt that utilizing art to document many of the stories recorded in the interviews could be a further way of helping not only the individuals who experienced the fires in some way but the larger community as well.

The special collections at the University of Tennessee Libraries are especially strong in the area of narrative illustration. A remarkable number of graduates from the university and others closely associated with it have had long and successful careers as cartoonists and/or editorial illustrators. The RFTA team applied for the Our Town grant, and in the summer of 2020 the NEA awarded that grant to commission illustrators to use the oral history archive to document and express the stories recorded therein. The four illustrators selected for this project, Paige Braddock, Charlie Daniel, Marshall Ramsey, and Danny Wilson, have had highly successful careers in illustration and, more importantly, deep ties to the mountains and the region. Braddock, Ramsey, and Wilson all used the archives as inspiration for the images they created. Daniel generously contributed two illustrations he created and published at the time of the wildfires. By bringing together these artists with the stories of the fire, we hope to have furthered the goal of the Our Town program.

The artists were not asked to tell the story of the wildfires. Consequently, this publication is not a graphic nonfiction narrative. Rather, the artists were asked to listen to as many interviews as they could and then use what they found in those interviews to express scenes, events, and feelings through their art that give illustrative representation to the experience of the wildfires. In many cases the artists did tie an image to a particular memory or story. In other instances, an image expresses a scene that stands for a larger feeling of the collective experience.

Our thanks to the NEA for supporting this effort to use illustration to further document the stories of the wildfires along with other activities involving the community and the artwork represented here. We also want to thank the City of Gatlinburg and the Anna Porter Public Library for their support and trust.

RISING FROM THE ASHES PROJECT TEAM
The University of Tennessee Libraries

Acknowledgments

THE UNIVERSITY OF TENNESSEE LIBRARIES WOULD LIKE TO THANK the many people involved in this project and its oral histories, and especially the artists who were inspired to give new form to the stories and experiences related in many of the interviews: Paige Braddock, Marshall Ramsey, and Danny Wilson. Additionally, Charlie Daniel graciously contributed two illustrations he created shortly after the fires. We would also like to thank the team who collected these interviews and who worked to make the archive available to the public: Jennifer Beals, Mark Baggett, Kaila Clark, Drew Edwards, Emily Gore, Chelsea Jacobs, Kelsey Jones, Casey Kaufman, Olivia Kelley, Holly Mercer, Margie Nichols, Christian David Rivera, Laura Romans, Steven Escar Smith, and Ken Wise. We would also like to thank the National Endowment for the Arts. The Our Town grant program funded not only the illustrations presented in this book but also outreach and engagement programs with the local community.

Introduction

RECEIVING UP TO 85 INCHES OF RAIN IN A NORMAL YEAR, the Great Smoky Mountains National Park is noted for being able to create its own damp weather like other temperate rainforests. The Smokies are so called because of the damp smoky-looking clouds that seem to cling to the mountaintops routinely. Because of this traditional dampness, the Great Smokies have very few forest fires. Yet, the events of late November 2016 were historic, even unprecedented.

A large portion of the Southeast—Tennessee, Georgia, Alabama, North and South Carolina—was experiencing either severe, extreme, or exceptional drought conditions. Many areas had only received a trace of rain for weeks during a time when September traditionally marks the end of summer with rainfall. On November 14, Tennessee governor Bill Haslam issued a burn ban for 51 counties. By November 15, the US Forest Service was tracking 33 wildfires throughout the region. Lightning or accidental human activity like campfires may have started many of the fires. Arson is blamed for others.

The original spark to the once-in-a-lifetime Great Smoky Mountains wildfire came on Wednesday, November 23, along the Chimney Tops trail. A popular path I have hiked many times. Months of drought had made the environs a tinderbox.

By the next day, the park service had delineated boundaries from natural features in the hope of encouraging the blaze to burn itself out. Three Chinook helicopters began dumping water on the rugged terrain that surrounds the Chimney Tops, and the fire that covered one acre smoldered for five days.

By Sunday, November 27, the weather report became ominous. Adding to what the National Oceanic and Atmospheric Administration (NOAA) already called an "exceptional" drought and a humidity level of only 17 percent, the National Weather Service predicted wind gusts of up to 40 mph the following day.

If our fate is controlled by the stars, then those stars were in total disarray Monday, November 28. The predicted winds blew into the foothills of Mount LeConte with gusts of up to 87 mph and created a firestorm that blew down and out of the national park like the demons in "Night on Bald Mountain" from Disney's *Fantasia*. Burning embers were tossed like confetti.

A second fire was soon reported north of the containment line at the Chimneys Picnic area south of the Sugarlands. High winds carried glowing fireballs due north around the Bullhead and into the LeConte Creek watershed to Mynatt Park, within Gatlinburg city limits. Guests and hotel employees at the nearby fifteen-story Park Vista Hotel were soon trapped. The lobby filled with smoke while they watched the flames pass their lofty vantage point and blaze over Turkeys Nest Road. From there it moved over the ridge of my boyhood adventures and down into Baskins Creek, my natal waters, where flames soon engulfed my childhood home on the hillside. No doubt, it burned in minutes. People caught upstream were forced to walk down Baskins Creek Road blocked by downed burning trees. The narrow watershed gorge had intense flames on both sides. But the firestorm did not stop there. It burned through to Silverbell, Roaring Fork, and Raccoon Ridge Roads and out Highway 321 toward Pittman Center. Fires raged down the Little Pigeon River and Gatlinburg Spur ultimately to the outskirts of Pigeon Forge.

But to lump the destruction into one giant fire would be misleading. Separate fireballs were falling in multiple places. Plus, the hurricane force winds were knocking down trees and power lines throughout the area. This cut off electricity and limited communications for town officials directing emergency responders. One such downed–power line fire burned 94 homes in Cobbly Nob subdivision a dozen miles northeast of Gatlinburg.

With spotty power outages, local communication became problematic. Firefighters found hydrants without water because of power loss at pumping stations. It is hard to imagine a more hellish scenario for one's hometown.

By 8 p.m. people were finally told to evacuate with word coming from Knoxville media or simply being passed door to door. Some were forced to walk out because of downed trees. Anxious callers overwhelmed the resort town's fire department and 911 service. Separate blazes found Chalet Village, where several people ultimately died, and raged down Campbell Lead into Greystone Heights. Scores fled, many on foot through the choking smoke trying to find their way out of the blazes via Wiley Oakley Drive.

"It's absolute hell," was a declaration made and echoed in various ways by several people caught in it.

Ultimately, the multiple fires destroyed or damaged 2,500 homes and buildings, killed 14 people, injured another 200 or more, and burned over 17,000 acres of mostly woodlands that were a powder keg of dried leaves— all in a matter of three hours.

Mercifully, rain began to fall around 11 p.m.

It was late December 2016. I had delayed the trip to Gatlinburg not knowing what I would find.

At 455 Baskins Creek Road, I walked around the burnt-out house on the hill slowly, through the grass I had mowed hundreds of times now charred, every single blade once green now black and brittle, past the basement door where my mother Helen had washed a gazillion loads of dirty clothes, around to the backyard where there once had been a garden, hives of honeybees, and a crude basketball goal attached to a sycamore tree, past my sister Darlene's bedroom where Nancy Drew had solved her mysteries, and then past the disability ramp I built for my father, Russell, after his quadruple bypass surgery in 1996, there at the back door into the kitchen where we had eaten so many biscuits.

It was all there yet crumbled into that crawlspace: the cabinets painted avocado by Mom, the coral and white bathroom tile, the knotty-pine walls nailed in place by Dad. All crumbled into that crawlspace, just ashes. The only thing still erect was the chimney made up of large, rounded cobbles carried up from the creek and the brick hearth, fireplace, and mantle where stockings had hung Christmas after Christmas for over thirty years.

Since they were married in 1949, my parents had spent their entire sixty-year marriage in that house. The house was built on land that had been given to them as a wedding present by Grandma Pearl after my father returned from the Navy and World War II. I had slept in the bedroom that overlooked the dogwood tree and "See Rock City" birdhouse, lived and ate there until I grew up and went away to college, with my sister following me two years later. But we returned every Christmas for two more decades. It was all there, ten thousand memories crumbled into that crawlspace.

Almost every week of the year you hear of such disasters that happen somewhere in the world due to tornados, hurricanes, mudslides, tsunamis, or fires that affect people's hometowns, homes, and livelihoods. As I write these words in early September 2021, New Orleans is dark after Hurricane Ida passed through just days ago, while California's Caldor wildfire has burned hundreds of homes and threatens 34,000 more in the Lake Tahoe area. And not that far from where I currently sit, a magnitude 7.2 earthquake violently shook the impoverished country of Haiti west of its capital, Port-au-Prince, killing hundreds.

You hurt for the people who lose so much so quickly. POOF! Lose everything. "The horror!" as Kurtz moaned in *Heart of Darkness*. But when it happens to your town, your neighborhood, your home, you cannot speak; you are in such a state of disbelief and shock, you are numb. You simply cannot cry. That will come later.

Perhaps Asheville's own Thomas Wolfe said it best, "You can't go home again."

But let me be clear. All I lost was the decades-old fountainhead of my memories, but I did not lose the memories. What has been collected here in this volume are the thoughts and feelings of so many, many people that lost so very much more.

I guess it's a good thing you only have one hometown to lose. You can only cry so many tears.

STEPHEN LYN BALES

Eighth generation Gatlinburgian

Pi Beta Phi Elementary School – Class of '65

Gatlinburg-Pittman High School – Class of '69

Author of three books published by The University of Tennessee Press: *Natural Histories*, *Ghost Birds*, and *Ephemeral by Nature*

Paige **Braddock**

Stacey Adam and Chris Szaton evacuated and were initially told that their house had burned. But when they were finally allowed to go back in, they realized their home was still standing. The burned-out foundations of their neighbor's houses surrounded it. They described the destruction as something like a war zone.

PAIGE 2021

Something I heard in multiple interviews was worry for visitors who weren't from the Gatlinburg area. Many tourists were visiting at the time of the fire, several people mentioned fears about those visitors finding their way out with so many roads closed or blocked. Charlie Anderson talked about one of his employees at the rental resort he manages and owns. He said this young man drove his pickup to lead several cars of visitors unfamiliar with the area out a dirt backroad to safety.

PAIGE 2021

Becky Jackson said she had found out about the fire while at work. She left to try and get to her house, but the police stopped her. She couldn't get to her house, and she couldn't get her husband to leave. Finally, she convinced him to leave and just bring her pets. Once he was down the mountain, the authorities wouldn't let him go back. Their house was destroyed by the fire.

Pets were mentioned in many interviews. Some people were able to evacuate with their pets. Some people left their pets behind thinking the fire wouldn't get close or because they were unable to take them along.

PAIGE 2021

Helen Barnett of Great Smoky Mountains Church of Christ in Pigeon Forge remembered how the church helped folks who had lost everything. Survivors would show up at the church in shock, just needing to talk. Helen and other volunteers at the church gave people food, blankets, whatever they could that might help. Listening to her talk made me imagine the church as a beacon, a safe haven in the community's hour of need.

Reporter Leslie Ackerson was by herself to do an 11:00 a.m. report from a neighborhood near the fires. She talked about how bad the air quality was and how the little kids had to stay inside during recess. At first, it was a small fire and people didn't know the fire could be a problem. It was still far away. The wind, dust, and leaves created hazy darkness by late afternoon.

PAIGE 2021

Stacey Adam and Chris Szaton packed bags and then worked all day cleaning leaves from gutters and lawn, showering their house with hoses—both the roof and grass around the house. At 6 p.m. someone came to the house and told them they had to leave now. Stacey mentioned her sense of empathy for her neighbors. Even though she and Chris didn't lose their house, the fire was a life-altering experience.

PAIGE 2021

PAIGE 2021

This is to illustrate a comment I heard in many interviews. People escaped with small things that they thought they cherished; and for those that lost so much, there was ultimately a realization that what really mattered most was the safety of loved ones . . . family and friends.

PAIGE 2021

In the aftermath of the fire John Schwartz and Salley Reamer did water and soil testing, wondering about the environmental impact of the fire, answering questions like what is the condition of the soil? Is the water safe to drink?

PAIGE 2021

Reporter Leslie Ackerson saw people packing up to leave. They were packing photo albums, paintings, and other precious things. One woman spoke to Leslie about having to leave her piano behind.

Evacuating for an imminent fire causes you to think about what has true meaning in your life. What you will bring and things you must leave behind.

Sometimes the things that you leave are just as meaningful, but too large to bring with you.

Seemona and Daniel Whaley kept watching the smoke, thinking the fire was still far away. Their cat hovered near the vents, apparently sensing the smoke coming in. Finally, they could see that one of the lodges below them was on fire. Someone called and told them to leave now. They had a hard time escaping, having waited almost too long to leave. A fallen tree that was on fire beside the road blocked the way out. They could see one of their friends' houses in flames.

Charlie Daniel

Marshall Ramsey

ON WEDNESDAY, NOVEMBER 23, 2016 at 5:30 P.M., THE CHIMNEY TOPS2FIRE WAS REPORTED IN THE GREAT SMOKY MOUNTAINS NATIONAL PARK. THE FIRE BURNED IN REMOTE TERRAIN, WITH VERTICAL CLIFFS and NARROW ROCKY RIDGES. THIS IS WHERE THE STORY BEGINS.

"NEVER IN THE HISTORY OF THIS PARK OR EVEN IN THE SURROUNDING AREA HAD ANYONE SEEN *the* COMBINATION *of* SEVERE DROUGHT, FIRE ON *the* LANDSCAPE, AND AN EXTREME WIND EVENT OCCURRING *at the* SAME TIME. IT WAS THE PERFECT STORM." JOE STRUTLER, USFS, WHO LED EIGHT PERSON TEAM *to* REVIEW *the* MANAGEMENT OF THE CHIMNEY TOPS 2 FIRE.

SMOKE FROM the CHIMNEY TOPS 2 FIRE SETTLED INTO the VALLEY, GIVING GATLINBURG AN OTHER WORLDLY APPEARANCE. STEPHANIE SWEENEY, NOTICING RAINING ASH, CALLED THE FIRE DEPARTMENT EARLY IN the AFTERNOON. "AT THIS POINT OF TIME, NO ACTIVE FIRES ARE IN GATLINBURG." NOTICING THE THICKENING SMOKE, SHE LOADED HER TWO SONS, DOG AND CAT, TOOTHBRUSHES AND TAX FORMS. WINDS, AT NEAR HURRICANE FORCE, WERE KNOCKING DOWN TREES. SWEENEY FOLLOWED HER INSTINCT TO LEAVE AND HEADED TO A FRIENDS HOUSE IN SEVIERVILLE.

BY 8 P.M., THERE WAS A MANDATORY EVACUATION CALLED FOR GATLINBURG. THE FLAMES WERE FLANKING DOWNTOWN. SINCE NOON, THERE WERE OVER 3,500 BOOTS ON the GROUND FROM 225 AGENCIES. BUT THE HIGH WINDS WERE RELENTLESS. FLAMES RAPIDLY ADVANCED. EVEN LONG-TIME RESIDENTS HESITATED to LEAVE THEIR HOMES. CITY MANAGER CINDY CAMERON OGLE'S HUSBAND, BUD, DID NOT INITIALLY EVACUATE. FINALLY HIS GRAND-DAUGHTER CONVINCED HIM to LEAVE. HE WENT to CHECK ON HIS MOTHER STELLA (SHE AND HER HUSBAND COOT WERE TOURISM PIONEERS. BUD TOLD HER, "OUR TOWN IS GETTING READY TO BURN DOWN." SHE LEFT WITH BUD. BUD AND CINDY, LIKE SO MANY, LOST EVERYTHING.

MASTER MENTALIST AND MAGICIAN ERIK DOBELL WOKE UP FROM A NAP TO FLICKERING LIGHTS. WHEN HE OPENED HIS FRONT DOOR, WHAT HE SAW WASN'T AN ILLUSION. "I OPENED THE DOOR AND EVERYTHING WAS ON FIRE. IT LOOKED LIKE CARTOON HELL." DOBELL GRABBED MONEY, HIS LAPTOP, A PHOTO ALBUM AND GOT OUT. "THERE WASN'T TIME TO THINK. HE HEADED DOWN SKI MOUNTAIN ROAD. THE CAR WAS HOT AND HE THOUGHT THE TIRES WOULD MELT. HE WAS FORTUNATE, "THE FIRE STOPPED AT MY DRIVEWAY. MY APARTMENT WAS SPARED." WHILE HE HAD NIGHTMARES AFTERWARD, HE COULDN'T SAY ENOUGH NICE THINGS ABOUT THE FIRE DEPARTMENT.

FAITH and FATE LINED UP the NIGHT OF the 28th. GARY & JILL OWNBY HAD SETTLED IN FOR THE NIGHT WHEN GARY WOKE UP TO SEE FIRE COMING OVER THE HILL. LOADING UP THE DOG, TWO GALLONS OF GAS AND HIS TRUSTY BOY SCOUT KNIFE, GARY AND JILL HEADED DOWN THE MOUNTAIN. SOON THEY CAME TO A FALLEN TREE ON THE POWERLINES. GARY CUT LIMBS OFF, REDUCING the TREES WEIGHT and ALLOWING THEIR CARS AND THEIR FRIENDS, TESSA'S CAR TO GET UNDER. TESSA, WITH the HELP OF A POLICE OFFICER, WAS THEN ABLE TO RESCUE HER 99-YEAR OLD GRANDMOTHER.

"NEVER IN the FIELD of HUMAN CONFLICT WAS SO MUCH OWED BY SO MANY to SO FEW." SIR WINSTON CHURCHILL. WITH FACES COVERED WITH SOOT AND BODIES EXHAUSTED to the CORE, FIRST RESPONDERS FOUGHT FLAMES IN the HILLS, WALKED HALLS of HOTELS AND CARRIED CITIZENS To SAFETY - EVEN WHEN THEIR OWN HOMES WERE IN PERIL.

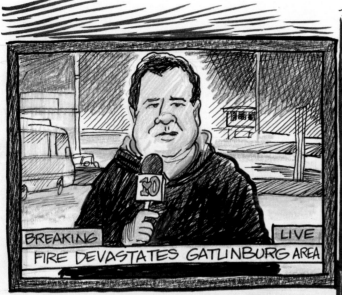

BREAKING   LIVE

FIRE DEVASTATES GATLINBURG AREA

LOCAL REPORTERS FOUND THEMSELVES COVERING AN INTERNATIONAL STORY. WBIR'S RUSSELL BIVEN, WHO HAD COVERED THE AREA FOR 20 YEARS, WORKED HARD NOT TO PASS ALONG RUMORS AND TO GET OUT WAYS FOR THE VIEWERS TO HELP. BUT IT WAS EMOTIONAL WORK. ALTHOUGH HE HAD COVERED KATRINA, THIS WAS DIFFERENT. THIS WAS HOME. AND THE WORLD WAS WATCHING. AT ONE POINT OVER 1,000,000 VIEWERS WERE WATCHING ON FACEBOOK. BIVEN REFUSED TO STAY IN A HOTEL. HE DIDN'T WANT TO TAKE A BED FROM AN EVACUEE. "I DROVE HOME EVERY NIGHT TO HUG MY FAMILY."

"AFTER DAY FOUR, I HAD TO GO HOME... WHERE I HAD A GOOD CRY."

14 CONFIRMED DEAD

WHEN IT WAS OVER, BIVEN WAS TIRED BUT COMFORTED KNOWING WHEN SOMETHING BAD HAPPENS IN EAST TENNESSEE, SOMEONE WILL HAVE YOUR BACK.

47

LATE MONDAY NIGHT, THE RAIN FINALLY ARRIVED AND LIKE THE FINAL SCENE IN A HORROR MOVIE, THE MONSTER WAS BEAT BACK. BY 6 A.M., THE OFFICIAL RAIN GAUGE IN GATLINBURG RECEIVED .73 OF AN INCH. EVERY DROP HELPED FIRE FIGHTERS CONTAIN the BLAZE. MORE RAIN WOULD COME IN THE FOLLOWING DAYS. IN HER ORAL HISTORY, GATLINBURG CITY MANAGER CINDY CAMERON OGLE SAID THAT WITHOUT the RAIN, "THE FIRES WOULD HAVE GONE TO DOUGLAS LAKE."

RECOVERY WAS A MARATHON, NOT A SPRINT. AT 11 P.M., RAINS CAME HELPING to TAME the FLAMES. TWO DAYS AFTER THE FIRE, DR. JACK PARTON, SEVIER CO. SCHOOL SUPERINTENDENT SAID, "THE REASON WE ARE GOING TO MAKE IT IS BECAUSE WE ARE MOUNTAIN TOUGH AND WE HAVE A STRONG FAITH IN JESUS CHRIST." MOUNTAIN TOUGH STUCK.

I CORINTHIANS 3:13

"WE JUST SAID A PRAYER FOR THANKFULNESS THAT WE STILL HAD EACH OTHER, THAT WE STILL HAD THE MEANS TO MOVE FORWARD AND TO MAKE A BETTER PATH FORWARD OUT OF THIS..." BOB SWEENEY to HIS SON STANTON (WHO TOOK the PHOTO THIS IS BASED ON)

THE U.S. DEPARTMENT OF COMMERCE'S NATIONAL INSTITUTE OF STANDARDS AND TECHNOLOGY SURVEYED 323 RESIDENTS. NINETY-FIVE PERCENT HAD NOT EVACUATED BEFORE. ONLY 18.3% HAD A HOUSEHOLD EMERGENCY PLAN PRIOR TO the FIRE AND 86.7% EVENTUALLY EVACUATED LAST MINUTE. BOB AND STEPHANIE SWEENEY, LIKE SO MANY IN GATLINBURG, LOST NEARLY EVERYTHING. IF YOU HAD to, QUICKLY EVACUATE, WHAT WOULD YOU BRING? (STEPHANIE SWEENEY FINDS HER GRANDMOTHER'S CAST IRON SKILLETS.)

"IT WAS LIKE A WAR ZONE," THAT'S HOW CHARLIE ANDERSON DESCRIBED HIS BELOVED TREE TOPS RESORT AFTER the FIRE. HE AND HIS WIFE GALE HAD BEEN CAMPING IN CHATTANOOGA WHEN FLAMES ROARED THROUGH GATLINBURG WITH LITTLE WARNING. ONE HUNDRED PEOPLE HAD BEEN IN OCCUPANCY; YET SOME HAD LEFT EARLY. THE ROAD FROM the PEDISTALS WAS BLOCKED. BUT ONE EMPLOYEE KNEW OF A BACK ROAD to 321, SAVING EVERYONE. THANKS to INSURANCE, TREE TOPS RESORT HAS BEEN REBUILT LIKE IT WAS BEFORE ($30 MILLION). CHARLIE ANDERSON SAID COVID WAS HARDER FINANCIALLY. HE PASSED AWAY ON APRIL 29, 2021.

1. SUSAN MELCHOR, WHOSE HOME WAS OFF FOX RUN, IS A CLASSIC EXAMPLE of HOW VOLUNTEER GROUPS HELPED VICTIMS REBUILD WHEN INSURANCE and OTHER AID FELL SHORT.

2. MONDAY MORNING, SHE NOTICED EMBERS FALLING FROM the SKY. SHE CALLED WORK TO SAY SHE NEEDED to CLEAN LEAVES. SHE CLEANED UP, TOOK A SHOWER. AT 6:30, SHE SAW A FIRE TRUCK at THE END of the ROAD.

3. A VOICE INSIDE HER HEAD TOLD HER

GET OUT!

SO SHE LOADED UP PICTURES and HER PETS and DID JUST THAT.

4. FOR MONTHS SHE HAD BEEN HEARING "FIRE!" IN HER HEAD. BY 7 P.M., SHE WAS SAFELY IN PIGEON FORGE.

Welcome to PIGEON FORGE

HER FRIENDS SAID "YOU'RE BEING SENSATIONAL." BY 8:30, HER NEIGHBORS SAID HER HOME WAS on FIRE.

5. "GOD PROTECTED US, EVEN THOUGH I LOST EVERYTHING."

SUSAN MELCHOR HAD ESCAPED the FIRE. BUT HER HOME, PURCHASED to ESCAPE FLORIDA HURRICANES, WAS GONE. THANKFULLY SHE AND HER SON (AND PETS) WERE SAFE.

ONE CRUEL IRONY - AN OLD STOVE, THAT WAS FEARED to BE A FIRE HAZARD AND BROKE DURING CLEANING A FEW DAYS BEFORE THE FIRE, WAS UNTOUCHED BY the FLAMES

Melchor

1. THE COST OF REBUILDING STUNNED SUSAN. ONE BID WOULD HAVE EATEN UP MOST OF HER INSURANCE MONEY AND BUSTED HER BUDGET.

THEN A GODSEND ARRIVED. MISSION GROUPS HELPING HIS HANDS AND CHURCH OF THE COVE FROM TOWNSEND ARRIVED. THE VOLUNTEERING PROFESSIONALS BUILT the BASEMENT FOR $25,000.

$88,000 FOR ONLY the BASEMENT

BIDS 'R' US

6. WHILE THANKFUL TO HAVE SHELTER, LIVING IN AN UNHEATED, LEAKY TRAVEL TRAILER GOT the BEST OF SUSAN MELCHOR. "YOUR HOME IS YOUR REFUGE AND I JUST WANT TO GO HOME."

I'M HOME!

8. THE FAITH AND GIVING SPIRIT DEMONSTRATED BY HELPING HIS HANDS (FROM VINCENNES, INDIANA) and CHURCH OF THE COVE FROM TOWNSEND REPRESENTED THE RECOVERY EFFORTS THAT HAPPENED AFTER FIRE. TENNESSEE LIVED UP TO ITS NICKNAME "THE VOLUNTEER STATE."
"I WASN'T ASKING FOR A HANDOUT. I WAS ASKING FOR A HAND UP...I WANTED HOPE."

9. LIKE the WILDFLOWERS in the BURN AREA HOPE and HOMES SPROUTED ANEW.

THE FIRE WAS AN EQUAL OPPORTUNITY DESTROYER. RICH, POOR, YOUNG, OLD, PUBLIC SERVANTS, FIRST RESPONDERS, BUSINESS OWNERS — ALL LOST HOMES. IN THE FLAMES. THE DEVASTATION WAS SO WIDESPREAD THAT INITIALLY EVEN CITY LEADERS HAD MOMENTS OF DOUBT. BUT ENCOURAGEMENT CAME IN PRIVATE MOMENTS. LONGTIME CITY MANAGER CINDY CAMERON OGLE, WHO LOST HER HOME CONFIDED TO MAYOR MIKE WERNER'S WIFE CINDY (WHO LOST A HOME and BUSINESS), "I CAN'T DO THIS." WERNER REPLIED, "YOU HAVE to DO IT. WE NEED YOU." THEN THEY PRAYED TOGETHER.

GARY OWNBY, A THIRD-GRADE TEACHER AT PI BETA PHI ELEMENTARY SCHOOL, SAID THAT AT ANY GIVEN MOMENT, CHILDREN WOULD BURST INTO TEARS. "WE DIDN'T DO HARD STUFF WE DID STUFF TO GET BACK TO A REGULAR ROUTINE." HE TREATED THE CHILDREN WITH KID GLOVES TO FIND NORMALCY. CARA PARKER, A CLINICAL SOCIAL WORKER AT THE HELEN ROSS McNABB CENTER SAID THOSE KIDS HAD LOST HOMES. BY JANUARY, SHELTERS HAD CLOSED AND PEOPLE LIVED IN MOTELS. WHEN SHE VISITED, SHE ENCOUNTERED STRESS. AS TIME WENT ON, MORE FAMILIES CAME IN FOR SERVICES BECAUSE THE TRAUMA CAUSED BY EVACUATION. THE GOOD NEWS? THE STIGMA OF GETTING HELP EVAPORATED.

IN A TIME WHEN SO MANY STEPPED UP to GIVE, NO ONE DID IT ANY BETTER THAN DOLLY PARTON. THE MY PEOPLE'S FUND GAVE $1000 PER MONTH to ABOUT 900 FAMILIES IMPACTED BY the FIRE FOR SIX MONTHS. BUT SINCE THEY HAD RECEIVED SO MANY DONATIONS, IT WAS UPPED to $5,000 the FINAL MONTH. THE PEOPLE of SEVIER CO. RECEIVED $12.5 MILLION.

IN MEMORY OF

ELAINE BROWN (81) • BRADLEY WILLIAM PHILLIPS (59) • MAY EVELYN NORRED VANCE (75) •
CONSTANCE REED (34) • CHLOE REED (12) • LILY REED (9) • ALICE HAGLER (70) •
JANET SUMMERS (61) • JOE SUMMERS (71) • JOHN TEGLER (71) • MARILYN TEGLER (70) •
PAMELA JEAN JOHNSON (59) • ROBERT A. HEJNY (65) • THE REV. ED TAYLOR (85)

HE HEALS the BROKENHEARTED
AND BINDS UP THEIR WOUNDS.
PSALM 147:3

Danny Wilson

Smoky Classroom Windows. Sarah Reagan interview. The day of the fire Sarah Reagan was trying to teach third grade at Pi Beta Phi Elementary School in Gatlinburg, but the children were distracted. The distant smoke was getting closer and thicker outside the school, clearly visible through their classroom windows. "Then I started getting frightened . . . It was changing very quickly."

Return of the Table Mountain Pines. Karen Hughes interview. Karen Hughes, UT professor working in population biology, was involved in observation and research of the post-fire Smoky Mountain plant life, including the table mountain pine trees which are unique to the Appalachian Mountains. "All the trees were blackened, but those that still stood and still had a little bit of needles up on top, we saw that the pine cones had opened and dropped their seeds."

The Kindness of Strangers. Stephanie Sweeney interview. "We were blessed in so many ways. Every place we went there were people there that wanted to pray with us, they wanted to hug us."

Fire Truck Warning. Jottie and Marie Hand interview.
Spotting a fire truck near his house Jottie went
through the woods and then stood on the footboard
talking to the driver. He was told, "We can't hook up
to this hydrant! We've got to get off the mountain!"

First Responders' Animal Rescues. Leslie Wereszczak interview. Heroic first responders during the fire were not only on the lookout for people and property, but pets also. The University of Tennessee College of Veterinary Medicine received multiple animals with serious burns that were rescued by first responders during the wildfires.

Motorcycle Descent. Buddy McLean interview. The night of the fire, the last two people to leave the Lodge at Buckberry Creek were a chef and an event manager. They decided to leave together, but one had a motorcycle he did not want to leave behind, so she followed him down the mountain with flames on both sides of the road. "To this day, he has PTSD."

Lone Cabin. Frances Fox Shambaugh interview. Frances Fox Shambaugh, who lost her home and extensive library in the fire, also had a rental house further up the mountain. They finally got to go up and assess the damage. "Strange. Everything around it burned, but it was still there."

News Updates. When asked, "Where did you go after being evacuated?" multiple interviewees told of going to stay with friends or family, out of immediate danger but still in the area. They kept up with what was going on by watching Knoxville TV stations' news coverage. Fearing the worst, but hoping for the best, they waited for some word from their neighborhoods.

Topper. Adesola Odunayo and Leslie Wereszczak interview. Both Odunayo and Wereszczak, who work at UT College of Veterinary Medicine, mentioned a particular cat named Topper. He was the most severely burned of nearly twenty "firecats" that were treated in Emergency Critical Care at UTCVM. Topper had severe face and foot pad burns, but "he was a trooper." He and his owner had a happy reunion three days later. Topper's story spread and resulted in a Facebook page for people to follow his recovery progress.

Only a Manual. Ann Fairhurst interview. Ann Fairhurst studied the effects of the fire on small businesses. She found that for the most part there had been no training of employees in disaster preparedness. If any thought at all had been given, it was just a manual on the shelf. "Most of them thought it could never happen."

Santa Biblia. Julia Rodriguez interview. Rodriguez told the story of a friend who, when evacuating, forgot her Bible . . . the place she kept her money. Her home was lost.

Church. From the interview with a pastor and friend who both talked about the joy of when they were able to gather in church again after the days of tragedy and uncertainty. The verse on the screen is a verse from the hymn "Amazing Grace" that reads:

Through many dangers, toils and snares,
I have already come;
'Tis grace hath brought me safe thus far,
And grace will lead me home.

About the Artists

PAIGE BRADDOCK is an artist, writer, and the Chief Creative Officer at Charles M. Schulz Creative Associates. She is best known for her Eisner-nominated comic strip, *Jane's World*, the first gay-themed comic work to receive online distribution by a national media syndicate in the United States. Braddock concluded the comic strip after a twenty-year run in 2018. She has illustrated several *Peanuts* children's books, and her graphic novels for children include the *Stinky Cecil* series and the *Peanut, Butter, and Crackers* books. She lives with her wife, Evelyn, and their two dogs and a cat in Sebastopol, California.

CHARLIE DANIEL is an editorial cartoonist whose career is a digest of more than fifty years of local and national politics. Editorial cartoonist at the *Knoxville Journal* from 1958 until its closure in 1992, Daniel has been adding his wry brand of wit and insight to the *Knoxville News Sentinel* ever since. In 2011, the beloved artist donated his entire collection of hand-drawn, original cartoons to the UT Libraries, inspiring the 1,500-piece Charlie Daniel Editorial Cartoon Collection now held by the Betsey B. Creekmore Special Collections and University Archives.

MARSHALL RAMSEY is a two-time Pulitzer Prize finalist whose cartoons are syndicated nationally and whose artwork, stories, and posts are frequently shared on social media. He got his cartooning start as a student at the University of Tennessee, Knoxville, working at campus newspaper the *Daily Beacon*. Ramsey is editor-at-large for *Mississippi Today*, a nonpartisan, nonprofit news and media company. He hosts the television program *Conversations* and a weekly radio program on Mississippi Public Broadcasting.

DANNY WILSON is a freelance illustrator based in Knoxville, Tennessee, who has worked in numerous styles and genres for nearly forty years. As a digital concept artist for event and experiential marketing, Wilson has created work for Disney, Warner Bros., Netflix, Amazon, Coca-Cola, HGTV, Taylor Swift, among others. His poster art gained notoriety with the 2017 and 2018 Chick-fil-A Kickoff Games, the "world's largest college football game" the Battle at Bristol, and the Official University of Tennessee 1998 National Championship. He has also worked as a magazine and newspaper illustrator and was recently commissioned to create athletics branding for the University of Tennessee Volunteers and the University of Tennessee–Southern Firehawks. Wilson graduated from the University of Tennessee in 1984 with a BFA degree.